DESTINATION
WHOLENESS
GOING BEYOND BROKENNESS

―⚜―

CYNTHIA CHIRINDA

Destination Wholeness: Going Beyond Brokenness
© 2025 by Cynthia Chirinda

All rights reserved. No part of this publication may be reproduced, stored in a retrieval system, or transmitted in any form or by any means—electronic, mechanical, photocopying, recording, or otherwise—without the prior written permission of the author.

First published in 2016 by Wholeness Incorporated, Harare, Zimbabwe
Updated edition published in 2025
Email: info@cynthiachirinda.com
Website: www.cynthiachirinda.com
Cover Design: Tapiwa Kahonde
Typesetting & Layout: Tapiwa Kahonde and Annie Nyamudzwadzuro
Scripture quotations, unless otherwise indicated, are taken from the Holy Bible, *(KJV) King James Version.*

All rights reserved. No part of this publication maybe reproduced, stored in a retrieval system, or transmitted in any form or by any means, without prior permission in writing of the publisher, nor be otherwise circulated in any form of binding or cover other than that in which it is published and without a similar condition including this condition being imposed on the subsequent purchaser.

ISBN: 978-1-77928-171-5

Contents

Endorsement v
Dedication. vii
Acknowledgements ix
Preface xi
Introduction xiii

Chapter 1: Whirlwinds, Hurricane and Storms 1

Chapter 2: What Happened to Your Dreams?. 7

Chapter 3: Sovereign Foundations. 13

Chapter 4: Kintsukuroi - Repairing with Gold 23

Chapter 5: Refuelling from Emptiness. 35

Chapter 6: Refreshing Waters. 49

Chapter 7: The Perfect Finish - From Success to Significance. 57

Chapter 8: New Beginnings Release and Let Go!. 69

Spiritual Reflections. 77

Endorsement

To know the author of "Destination Wholeness" is to know a substantial woman, who is constantly on a journey to discover the enlightenment of being whole. As suggested in this title, it's a journey with no firm "journey's end". I was intrigued that there could exist such a blueprint, such a road map, or should I say a GPS, so able to assist us to negotiate the curves, turns and up hills that all our life's journeys will take us on. Cynthia's deep spiritual and intuitive understanding of tests and trials, and then her ability to offer simple and applicable day to day insight has immense power to be life changing. This book will now take place of pride on my bedside, as one of those well-read books of constant referral for me. An African solution to our unique African challenges, as written by one of the most outstanding young and influential women of our current time. It is timeous in its relevance to the changing mindset of our continent's shape shifters and game makers.

I would urge any person who is presently concerned with the content of their life, anyone who wants to fill the empty spaces along their journey to make a copy of "Destination Wholeness" their journeys handbook. May the richest blessings of our God continue to enlighten you and may you never lose your courage to put your thoughts to pen and paper.

Congratulations Cynthia!

Ana Scott - *Realtor, Motivational Speaker and Trainer*

This endorsement is reprinted in honour and memory of the late Ana Scott—a voice of faith, insight, and unwavering encouragement.

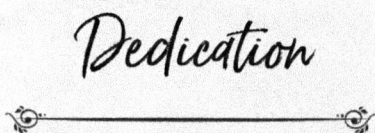

This book is dedicated to every soul that has gone through brokenness and came out strong on the other side.

Acknowledgements

To Pastor Yvonne Brooks, thank you for encouraging me to pursue the sequel to my first published book, *The Whole You*.

To Ddruooe Renders—an amazing cheerleader—thank you for the long emails, cyber hugs, and your honest and generous feedback on the book's concept and imagery when this journey began in 2014.

To Ana Scott—your life was a gift, and your encouragement lives on. Your words remain a treasured part of this book's legacy.

To my precious children and the village of support that has surrounded me through every season—I am deeply grateful for your love, grace, and presence. Your light has helped me find my own over and over again.

To every reader, mentor, friend, and silent intercessor—thank you for believing in the voice God placed in me and for walking alongside the message of wholeness.

To those across the globe who have followed my journey, quoted my reflections, shared my work, or whispered a prayer in silence—I see you, I honour you, and I thank you. May this book serve you as a companion of truth, healing, and realignment.

Preface

In 2005, after finalizing the manuscript for my book *The Whole You: Vital Keys for Balanced Living*, I nearly decided against publishing it. Something stirred within me—an awareness that there was still more to wholeness than balance alone. That moment became a spiritual checkpoint on a longer journey.

Over the years, through my work as a transformation catalyst and guide, I've encountered not only the complexity of the human experience, but also the silent undercurrents that shape how we engage life, purpose, and identity. I've come to realize that our pursuit of balance can feel empty and exhausting if we don't understand the deeper *why* of our journey—the foundation, the vision, and the destination.

The Whole You addressed the multidimensional nature of our being. *Destination Wholeness* goes deeper—to the inner infrastructure. It interrogates the root causes that keep us stuck in survival mode and hinder us from walking in the fullness of our calling. My understanding of wholeness has evolved from an external pursuit of balance to an internal awakening of alignment.

This book is written with that evolution in mind. It is not a manual. It is a mirror. A movement. A moment of invitation to unravel what's been hidden, heal what's been avoided, and rebuild what's been waiting for you.

The "Contemplative Moments" at the end of each chapter offer space for reflection, prayer, and courageous action. My hope is that you will not just read this book, but that you will *respond*—not to me, but to the voice of wholeness rising within you.

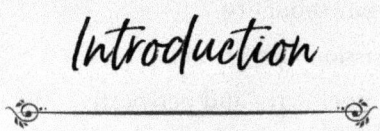

Introduction

Every day, we make decisions—some are routine and barely felt, others disrupt everything we thought we knew. Low-level decisions are preference-based. High-level ones? They cut deep. They define us. They're not always logical, but they are always revealing.

High-level decisions demand more than intellect. They pull truth from the soul.

Powerful decisions rarely lead us down the conventional path. Instead, they require us to honour our values and respond to an inner call that often feels countercultural. These decisions become life enactments of who we are—and who we are becoming.

"Wilt thou be made whole?"—John 5:6

The question Jesus asked the man at the pool of Bethesda remains a timeless challenge.

It is a question of **will**. Do you want to be made whole? Do you believe your brokenness does not disqualify you from purpose?

Wholeness begins where excuses end and courage begins. It's not about ignoring pain—it's about converting it. Spring may feel distant when you're still living in the chill of winter, but for those with engaged faith, *a shift is already in the atmosphere.*

Contemplation—though often overlooked in our fast-paced world—is essential to transformation. The pause is not passive. It is powerful. In those quiet moments, we discover what we've been too busy to face.

This book invites you into those pauses—moments of spiritual excavation and renewal. In this journey, you will be asked to:

- **Restructure** your thoughts
- **Refuel** your passion and dreams
- **Refresh** your inner drive and perspective

Can you trust God with your pain?
Can you see purpose beyond your wounds?
Can you believe that your healing will heal others?

Let this not just be a book, but a turning point.

Welcome to your *Destination Wholeness!*
Cynthia Chirinda

DESTINATION
WHOLENESS
GOING BEYOND BROKENNESS

Chapter One

Whirlwinds, Hurricanes and Storms

Growing up in the beautiful, deep rural lands of Chivhu in Zimbabwe I vividly remember how the boisterous winds before a wild storm would violently sweep through our homestead sending the chickens scuttling away in peril. Dishes flying away from the drying table and leaves getting caught up in the whirlwinds swirling away to the next homestead. Mother hens would quickly gather the little chicks into their protective embrace. The little children would run to hide behind their mother's skirts whilst the adventurous ones would be daring enough to chase after the whirlwind totally oblivious of the masses of dust whilst chanting away *"Chamupupuri chauya"* (the whirlwind has come) with such excitement and glee. The elders who believed there were spirits in the wind, would quickly chide this group of daring young ones with threats of being carried away into oblivion by the whirlwind and never to return. The obedient ones would heed to the call of the elders but the adventurous ones would keep running with excitement chasing the whirlwind and some of them secretly hoping to be taken away to a faraway dreamland for new experiences.

A whirlwind is a weather phenomenon in which a vortex of wind—(a vertically oriented rotating column of air), forms due to instabilities and turbulence created by heating and flow (current) gradients. Whirlwinds occur all over the world and in any season. Hurricanes, cyclones, and typhoons are all the same weather phenomenon, Scientists just call these storms different things depending on where they occur. On January 24 2011, Peter A. Adeosun in his blog *A Word for Today*, recounts how Friday, the 13th of August, 2004 was a day that he cannot easily forget. He narrates how he had just relocated with his family to Fort Myers on the west coast of Florida less than 3 weeks and on this particular day, the hurricane Charley made landfall in the area with maximum sustained wind speed at about 150 mph; a very dangerous category four hurricane! He says that he remembers how he and his wife together with their 10 month old baby huddled in the closet praying as the wind blew trees and poles and roofs fell all around. Peter says that their building was dangerously shaken to the foundations, they were not sure if the building they were in would stand as it felt as though it would fall at any time just like the other buildings they saw around them. He remarks how they survived and how they held on to their faith in what was one of the most costly hurricanes in the US history in terms of destruction and lives lost.

BATTLING WITH THE BOISTEROUS, CONTRARY WINDS OF LIFE

Matthew 14:22-32 gives an account of how Jesus made His disciples get into the boat and go before Him to the other side, while He sent the multitudes away. Studying the story of the disciples on this boat battling a boisterous wind that was blowing against them, one cannot but wonder why Peter would ask Jesus to have him come on the water at such a precarious moment. It was already very dangerous being on the boat and considering Peter's statement, he was not even completely sure it was the Lord. Peter trusted, jumped out of the boat and started walking on the water to go to Jesus.

There are several lessons that we can learn from this story. The first is that Jesus actually made His disciples get into this boat and indirectly into the situation. He did not bring it upon them but He allowed them to go through it. It was a very fearful experience for them; they were not sure that they would make it out alive. It is like receiving the report of a diagnosis that is life threatening, you are not sure if you are going to survive it - it could be very fearful. As these early disciples did, we will face storms and contrary winds blowing against us at some point that has nothing to do with whether we are believers living for God or not.

WHOLENESS AND LIFE'S STORMS

Wind of adversity is not peculiar to any one person. The wind did not blow against Peter only, or John only; it blew against all of them! We may not all be facing the same challenges, but we are all facing something that we need divine intervention for and as we trust Him, He will come through for us. Even though the winds of life may terrify us, sift us and relocate us, the decision to find wholeness lies deep within us. 'Wholeness' is generally defined as the state of being perfectly well in body, soul (mind, will and emotions) and spirit. It is complete sanctification and restoration according to God's original design for man before sin entered the world. According to the Miriam Webster Dictionary, "Wholeness is the condition of being sound in body. The quality or state of being without restriction, exception, or qualification." Sometimes life's challenges which uproot us and shake us like hopeless particles in the whirlwind can leave us feeling so fragmented and without any strength to gather ourselves again from feeling disjointed to becoming whole. So where do you find wholeness before, during and after the whirlwind? When we learn to surrender our lives to God and yield to His leading in the same way that the disciples trusted Jesus to ensure their safe passage to the other side, we will have begun the journey to a life of wholeness.

CONTEMPLATIVE MOMENTS:
READ THROUGH AND REFLECT BEFORE THE ACTION

The whirlwind violently gathers any vulnerable thing that it comes into contact with and consumes it within its force into whatsoever direction it pleases. It can uproot the foundations of precious, valuable things that took a lifetime to build. Where do you go when the contrary winds of life beat against you? What is your place of refuge and how safe is it? Who do you talk to and how do you encourage yourself until the wind passes?

My commitments for this week: I COMMIT to _____
_____
_____

My affirmations: I AM _____
_____
_____

My transformative actions this month: I WILL _____
(1) _____
(2) _____
(3) _____

Chapter Two

What Happened to Your Dreams?

Do you remember the day when you were young, hopeful and full of life? When you saw everything through the eyes of possibility and only wished you were a bit taller, bigger, stronger, or more powerful to take the world? Do you ever look back and wonder what happened to that person? We all come into this life with a positive view of the world. We were excited and imaginative, and we saw the entire universe as our playground. Then somewhere between high school graduation and middle-age, many seem to lose that optimism for life. Perhaps this stems from telling ourselves that we have to "grow up" and become more realistic. Or perhaps it is caused by those doubts that creep in our heads, making us wonder if we are just not good enough to ever become all those things we dreamt about. Or could it simply be the result of running ourselves ragged trying to meet the demands of those around us? Whatever the cause, we began creating barriers and limitations for ourselves that caused us to either try, fail, and give up; or even more prevalent, caused us not to try at all. Sometimes we still hear voices from our childhood days that chided us and restrained us for the sake of our protection. Could we have magnified those voices beyond reason to a place of paralysis? Decades later sadly some of those voices are still rehearsed in our subconscious and have created invisible prison walls for us where we dreadfully fear to step out into the unknown. At some point we became afraid, and we let that fear stop us.

The Fear Factor

Fear has a way of keeping us subdued and tucking us away in the background. It convinces us that we can never accomplish our dreams, tells us to maintain our silence, and often separates us from the ones we love. Fear has an unparalleled ability to freeze us in our tracks, and limit what we are willing to try. Fear makes us lead a smaller life. Tough moments in life can be anything from illness, losing your job, a dysfunctional relationship or acute lack. It is Victor Hugo who once said, "Courage is not the absence of fear, but the mastery of it." How do you master courage when the going gets tough?

It is easy to ignore our fears and hope that they will just go away. Unfortunately, they rarely do. If you do not face your fears, they will end up controlling you. How do you master the courage to face your fears? The most common way to face your fears is through exposing them to revelation and truth. You can start by making a list of your fears. You have to know what scares you. Sit down and draw up a list of things you are afraid of. What are their origins? When do they seem to crop up? When do they seem not so bad? How do they make you feel? Getting away from the fear and away from yourself as you look at yourself on paper will help you to be a bit more logical and objective about your fear. You then need to differentiate between rational and irrational fears. In some situations, it is perfectly natural to feel some level of fear. A healthy fear response is an evolutionary advantage that's helped humans survive in a hostile world for thousands of years. However, other fears are more irrational, and it is often these fears that can cause the most difficulty and distress. It is important to establish that fear in itself is not a bad thing as it exists for our protection and works as an early warning signal. There is however a big difference between the healthy fear that tells us to keep away from getting burnt and a constant fear that keeps us from living our life. Beyond dreaming again we need to strengthen our spiritual muscle and like the phoenix rise up again, recruiting support where necessary and start to step out towards our destiny with boldness.

ARISE FROM YOUR CONDEMNATION

So many people struggle with incessant self-condemnation. In self-condemnation your own voice is internalised and you use self-talk that comments negatively on your value, person-hood, actions, feelings and behaviour. In self-condemnation common negative self-talk experiences such as "You are stupid, unacceptable, weak, unworthy, a fraud, you are unlovable, a failure and not forgiven," often prevail in one's internal vocabulary.

Condemnation is a common condition which we all inevitably encounter. One of the most common symptoms is a feeling of oppression and bondage. It is an extremely oppressive burden which "beats us down." It is often accompanied by a nagging sense of guilt and it produces frustration, fear, insecurity, despair, defeat, and discouragement. It torments us with intense feelings of hopelessness and inferiority. There are several reasons why we can experience condemnation which vary from poor self-esteem, an improper view of God, the condemnation of others, failure, self-punishment to unresolved guilt from the past. Whilst some condemnation can be a result of our own errors and poor judgment, in some instances there are people who have been abused and as a result are constantly depressed. They continue to hold themselves accountable, blaming themselves and denying themselves of blessings that come with fulfilling relationships because they cannot release themselves from this self-condemnation

BROKENNESS AND PAIN SUBSTITUTES

Brokenness hurts! Brokenness can take many forms. It may include insignificance, emptiness, excessive anxiety, bitterness, depression, addictions, persistent shame, obsessive thoughts, compulsive behaviours, and even perfectionism. People who suffer from perfectionism simply cannot live up to their own expectations. All over the world people attempt to overcome pain by filling their lives with substitutes. These substitutes include alcohol, drugs, sex, material things, and even work. The main idea is to numb the pain with something else. Usually people hope to avoid pain with these substitutes. However, most of these substitutes only increase feelings of brokenness, hopelessness, and lead to lower self-esteem.

If we attempt to lift ourselves out of brokenness and become whole without turning to God, we will fail. We may, to be sure, be able to improve our lot in life, but complete wholeness is not possible. In order to overcome our brokenness we must realize that we have to be healed by a power greater than ourselves. If we look only to ourselves, we will not be able to make the journey from brokenness to wholeness. We need to believe and understand that God is not the author of our condemnation. It is not His will that we suffer condemnation in any form. Self-condemnation robs us of our joy and undermines our peace and confidence in Christ. In Romans 8:1(NKJV) we are reminded that "there is therefore now no condemnation to those who are in Christ Jesus, who do not walk according to the flesh, but according to the Spirit."

Wholeness is what we want and need to achieve our dreams and goals. In order to be whole, we have to be reconciled to God through Christ. Jesus will not impose His healing upon us. We must make the decision to turn to Him for healing. According to John 10:10b (KJV), Jesus said: "I am come that they might have life, and that they might have it more abundantly." This abundant life does not always shield us from brokenness, but it will help us through the dark seasons and give us victory.

CONTEMPLATIVE MOMENTS:
READ THROUGH AND REFLECT BEFORE THE ACTION

What do you see now when you close your eyes? What images dance before you and are you able to see any light beyond the shadows? Do you feel tormented when you close your eyes or do you feel reflective and at peace with your mind? What has kept you where you are - paralysed and fearful to make a move ahead? What are you going to do to confront it?

My commitments for this week: I COMMIT to _____
_____
_____

My affirmations: I AM _____
_____
_____

My transformative actions this month: I WILL _____
(1) _____
(2) _____
(3) _____

Chapter Three

Sovereign Foundations

Paralysed by Fear

I was born as the fifth and last child of my parents during the war era in Rhodesia. I was born at Mtoro rural clinic where my mother was a nurse near our farm in Chivhu. During that time, my father operated a vibrant General Dealer Store and a grinding mill in Mtoro, a few kilometres away from our homestead. This was at the height of the liberation war when the air was always pregnant with tension as the comrades sought refuge in the rural homesteads and villages at night where they would also be fed. It was during that time that the Rhodesian army lieutenant descended upon our homestead in the cool of the day demanding to see my father. A spot in the bush nearby had become a night base for the comrades where they would come for their change of clothes and rations of corned beef and beverages from the store. My father who had been faithfully taking care of the gallant sons was sold out by a neighbour (who was also a relative) for feeding the comrades with corned beef. Years later I could still hear the loud bark of the commanding officers as they turned our homestead upside down searching for my father on that day. "Where is Chirinda?" they continued to ask threateningly as they paced around the homestead with the guns and radios. Everyone knew that the narrative to give to the soldiers was that he had gone away to Harare to order stocks for the shop but on that day they had come in their hordes, surrounded the farm and searched every nook and cranny as they sought after my father who had slipped into the spare bedroom and lay under the bed for hours barely breathing for fear of being caught. Years later my father would always recount this particular incidence as one of the most fearful days of his life where he never thought he would escape. Even though these events took place in the very early years of my childhood, the trauma that registered in my subconscious made me freeze whenever I would see or hear the sound of army trucks. Years later when I had eventually moved to Harare, I would become so terrified every Wednesday morning when the garbage trucks would drive through our neighbourhood collecting garbage. Whilst the other younger children of my age would go around chasing the truck excitedly chanting *"Madhodhabhini, Madhodhabhini!"* (Garbage/refuse collectors), I would literally freeze in my tracks and hold my ears firmly shut as fear entered and paralysed my little body. The dread, peril and trauma consumed me yet again because of the sound association I had in my mind of the loud engines of the army trucks with the garbage trucks.

Clinton's Leadership Emergence Theory

Are leaders born or made? Or both? Leighton Ford noted in the Foreword to J. Robert Clinton's book on The Making of a Leader: Recognizing the Lessons and Stages of Leadership Development (1988), "I believe we can make either of two opposite mistakes in viewing leadership development. One is to attach a mystique to leadership that says in effect, 'God calls leaders. Leaders are born. There is nothing we can do about it.' The opposite is to say, 'Leaders are made. With the right techniques, we can produce them.'" (p. 10). It is true that God anoints certain leaders, such as Moses, David, Samuel, and Isaiah, calling them for a special purpose and setting them apart, exalting some and bringing down others (Psalm 75:6-7). At the same time, it is also true that there are processes that God uses to grow up leaders through developmental phases, as can be observed in the same biblical leaders as mentioned above. After years of research on the lives of historical, biblical and contemporary leaders across many fields, Dr. Clinton has observed a general pattern of development over the course of a leader's lifetime. He has identified specific stages within the leadership development process, as well as certain processes or experiences that God tends to use to promote growth at each stage. Known as the Leadership Emergence Theory, Clinton's theory of leadership development is outlined in six stages or phases which are:

Phase 1: Sovereign Foundations (Preparational Foundations)
Phase 2: Inner-Life Growth (Early Leadership Years)
Phase 3: Ministry Maturing (Middle Leadership Years)
Phase 4: Life Maturing (Later Leadership Years)
Phase 5: Convergence (Finishing Well)
Phase 6: Afterglow (The Wise Elder/Sage)

In this book we shall primarily focus on the first phase in the Leadership Emergence Theory which is Sovereign Foundations. Sovereign Foundations are about the early years of our lives, with all the circumstances, events, and significant people which impact us, often in ways over which we have no say or control. Which one of us chose our birth parents? Who among us had the opportunity to select our birth order, or gender, or country or region of birth? Who decided which primary school we went to, and even then, who would be our teachers? Did we request that bully to come and make our life miserable? Did we invite the drought, flood, fire, or illness to invade our family and disrupt it so? When did we elect to be born into a family of wealth—or poverty—or somewhere in the middle?

All of these items describe circumstances that are completely beyond our control, and yet which have had significant impact on our lives. We are shaped by these events, and sometimes these realities and incidents, even relationships, open or close opportunities available to us in the future. But whatever our circumstances, God has been there with us since before we were born, and God uses all of these events and experiences to shape us and prepare us for the good plans he has for us. Not only this, but we are each uniquely created. We all, each and every one of us, are made in God's image (Genesis 1:26-27). Among other aspects, this means we are thinking, feeling, and creative beings, made to function within relationships, with the ability to work with authority. This is true for each one of us. At the same time, we are each unique, with specific gifts, talents, temperaments, personalities, and wills.

God has created us, given us life, and placed us within human history at a particular time and place. We are not a mistake. As Clinton remarks, "God providentially works through family, environment, and historical events. This begins at birth....Keep in mind that it is often difficult to see the importance of all these items until later phases" (p.44). In this first phase of leadership development, though the prospective leader has little control over what happens, his or her primary lesson is to learn to take advantage of the situations presented, and to respond positively and proactively. Whatever our circumstances, how we respond is our responsibility, and is what shapes us. If we respond negatively, we tend to withdraw, blame, and perhaps become bitter and defeated, allowing our past to limit and bind us. If we respond positively, we grow in integrity, wisdom, vision, and influence. By responding positively, our character, personality, and underlying values are shaped, and we move in the direction of our destiny, the part we get to play in God's bigger plan.

I believe that we are all called to lead in one form or fashion, in some sphere and at some level of influence in the journey of our lives. In Sovereign Foundations, you can observe how God has shaped an individual, taught lessons, and laid the groundwork for the individual's future qualities, interests and contributions. In these first number years in a leader's life, many events, realities, individuals and circumstances significantly shape the person of the leader, most often in ways that are beyond one's control or choice. The key is how the individual has reacted to those early years, and what he or she does with them in the future.

Reflecting on my Sovereign foundations—My Journey

Growing up in the uniquely challenging situation that I found myself in at a very young age made me extremely vulnerable to abuse and neglect. This grew in me an independence and a coping mechanism to think beyond the pain.

I encountered several health attacks, most of which were spiritual in nature because of the deep traditional background that my elders in the family subscribed to. As a result I developed a deep understanding of the spiritual realm and the power of worship at a very young age. Because of the domestic economic situation, I was limited materially and faced major emotional challenges as I tried to fit into city life coming from a rural background, barely able to communicate in a single word of English. For several years I had to deal with self-esteem issues and did many things to find acceptance within communities of friends. Years later, I realised that since no one was going to affirm me I had to motivate myself and develop confidence in my abilities. This led me to a pursuit of self-discovery and eventually finding my purpose in God in during my school years. I then found completeness and hence my passion for assisting people to find their purpose in God. I faced a lot of false accusations as I was growing up and no matter how much I avoided people and situations I would somehow find myself wrongly accused in issues I had no idea about. Today this has helped me not to judge people based on hearsay until I also hear their side of the story. There was a lot of humiliation and bullying around me at this early stage which affected my self-esteem. At this stage in my life I became a very deep thinker and enjoyed prolonged moments of solitude. As someone who was given to deep thinking I developed an ability to design schemes and strategies, both positive and negative.

From Sovereign Foundations to Life Maturing: Lessons Learnt

In the sovereign foundations phase I developed a stewardship and shepherding spirit from taking care of the flocks which were our primary wealth base. Cattle, goats and sheep each require a different technique to herd them yet each time you have to keep a watchful eye on them so that they do not stray as you lead them to pastures. I developed knowledge of managing scarce resources, survival skills, and an attitude of humility. Even though I did not have an intimate knowledge of God I developed a dependency and trust in

Him because I knew that He alone understood the pain I was going through as a result of the rejection and abuse I suffered during my early childhood years. I was also exposed to spirituality in traditional ancestral practices which gave me an understanding of how the spirit world operated.

Throughout my high school years I was elected into several leadership positions and in my fourth year I was awarded a coveted leadership trophy. It was during these years that I developed grooming, deportment and etiquette skills through the school system. Towards the end of my high school came my first major leadership assignment when I was appointed head girl of my school. This is when I knew that God had cut me out for leadership as I operated under a unique unction with authority and wisdom which could only have been God-given. I was blessed with a unique set of capable individuals in the Prefects body and an amazingly supportive administration and staff. I excelled in my sportsmanship and literary skills majoring in the arts of public speaking, debate, drama writing and acting in English, Shona and French. High school life was a capacity building experience for me. I learnt discipline through the rigorous military style training I underwent when I was recruited for the Zimbabwe Under-20 Volleyball team and as I trained with other volleyball clubs apart from our school team which participated in various tournaments countrywide. My self-image and confidence was built throughout my high school years through teachers and school mates who always seemed to see great and beautiful things in me. During this Inner-Life Growth phase also referred to by Clinton as the Early Leadership Years, my faith began to build me up and I began to embrace the truth that I belonged to God and I was but clay in his hands hence I reached a healthy level of surrender in the midst of persecutions from various angles.

Having started out my working career as a high school teacher, the passion and gift to impart knowledge and skills manifested deeply in my Ministry Maturing middle leadership years. When I later moved to the corporate world pursuing a career in marketing communications and human resource development, I developed a wealth of corporate management skills which I still use today in my consultancy work.

From the time I gave my life to Christ in 1991, I also received the baptism of the Holy Spirit and began to develop my spiritual gifts in the area of teaching, exhortation and word of wisdom. Over the years these gifts have matured and I have had the opportunity to exercise them in ministry, in the market place and in nation building initiatives. During the ministry maturing phase of my life I learnt to seek out for inner healing from God because of the series of challenges I faced in my relational life. I have also developed an ability to receive and relay instructions from God for ministry through writing, teaching and praying. It has been a journey of consolidating my gifts and experiences for use in the body of Christ, in organisations and in developing individuals for nation building.

In my life maturing phase I became actively involved in ministry at various levels and to date I have been able to exercise and strengthen the gifts of exhortation, leadership, teaching, wisdom and administration amongst others on several platforms beyond our church walls. My passion for strategy, organizational structuring and leadership has helped me to train groups, produce materials, publications, film productions as well as helping authors to publish their work to date. God has started to increase my reach into national institutions within Africa.

What is your story? How have you survived this long? Of all the trials and tribulations you faced, you have survived and can turn those circumstances into stepping stones and building blocks.

CONTEMPLATIVE MOMENTS:
READ THROUGH AND REFLECT BEFORE THE ACTION

In the first phase of our lives, Sovereign Foundations, we all face challenges and opportunities which shape our future leadership.

We may or may not have significant physical limitations, but we all face challenges and opportunities which shape our future leadership. As you reflect on your life from before birth, your childhood, and through your teen years, consider the following questions:

1. What was the family situation that you were born into? What was your birth order, and what role did you tend to play in the family?
2. What challenges did you face when you were small, and how did they contribute to whom you are today? (Certain events, illnesses, physical limitations, people, disappointments, problems…)
3. How did you tend to respond to challenges when you were young? How do you respond to those same challenges today, as you think back about them?
4. Who were significant people who shaped you during your early years, either negatively or positively? How did they shape you? (Teaching you what you did not want to become, giving you positive encouragement through something they did or said, serving as a role model, etc.)

My commitments for this week: I COMMIT to _____
_____
_____

My affirmations: I AM _____
_____
_____

My transformative actions this month: I WILL _____
(1) _____
(2) _____
(3) _____

CHAPTER FOUR

Kintsukuroi – Repairing with Gold

Once upon a time, in the far, far east, east even of Eden, lived a great emperor, in a great palace, gorgeously stocked with the richest of goods. It was early spring, and the season of royal visits, when kings and princes called on one another and admired each other's choicest possessions, gave wonderful gifts and enjoyed bountiful banquets. And this year was special, because the visitors would see the investiture of his beloved son Kintsukuroi as Crown Prince of the empire.

The emperor was excited this year because he had a new and beautiful bowl to show to his friends, specially made for him by the finest of craftsmen from the finest of materials. Imagine then his horror when on going to his cabinet he discovered that it was broken apart, into a hundred pieces. How could it have happened? No-one knew. What could be done about it before the first visitors arrived? No-one could offer any idea, for the time was too short to start again and make another one.

The emperor was dismayed, sad that he could not show off his beautiful bowl, but even sadder that something so beautiful should have broken. He retired into his private apartments with only his beloved son to share his sorrow, and they talked long into the night together.

Next morning the emperor woke to the sound of a great commotion. His senior ministers demanded to see him urgently. The cabinet of treasures had now been broken into, and this time the great new golden diadem that had been made for his beloved son, ready for the investiture, was quite simply gone—along with the broken pieces of the broken bowl, but who cared about those now.

What is more, the thief had been seen, but not recognized, since he was covered in dirt and scars, with nothing to distinguish him from a thousand other down-and-outs who hung around the palace, for the emperor—to the annoyance of his ministers—refused to turn them out but shared his food with them.

No-one knew for sure where the thief had gone, but he had, they thought, run off towards the princes apartments. There the doors were most unusually now locked and there was no answer to their knocking, though they could hear sounds inside. Would the emperor give his permission for them to break down the door: they dare not act without it!

The emperor was silent for many minutes. On his face his ministers saw sadness but not anger, lament but also love. What was going on? Eventually the emperor spoke. "Leave the prince and his apartments alone. If he is ready to rule, he must be allowed to act. His will and my will are as one." The ministers were not at all sure just what this meant, but the message was clear. They were to do precisely nothing.

So the day passed. The emperor remained in his private apartments. Those of the prince remained locked, though smoke could be seen coming out of the chimney and a fire had obviously been lit. And eventually the ministers tired of their waiting and went to bed. The important guests were expected the very next day.

Imagine now their surprise in the morning when they went to the treasure cabinet to prepare its items for display and found the precious bowl back in its place, whole again, but glistening with veins of gold where the cracks had been. Its beauty seemed all the greater. And by it the prince's crown, a slim band now, but speaking in its simplicity of a strength, an authority all the more striking, because it had given itself away and given glory to another, but was the greater itself for it. The investiture could go ahead.

A smile of secret understanding passed between the emperor and the son whose newly scarred hands had shown him worthy to come into the kingdom. (The Fable of Kintsukuroi is an original composition by David Thomson, Bishop of Huntingdon)

More Beautiful Than the Original

Kintsugi or *kintsukuroi* is a Japanese method for repairing broken ceramics with a special lacquer mixed with gold, silver, or platinum. The philosophy behind the technique is to recognize the history of the object and to visibly incorporate the repair into the new piece instead of disguising it. The process usually results in something more beautiful than the original. Kintsukuroi means 'to repair with gold' in Japanese, and beyond the art of repairing pottery with gold there is an understanding that the piece is the more beautiful for having been broken. In Japan, instead of tossing valuable broken pieces in the trash, some craftsmen practice this 500-year-old art of *kintsugi*, or "golden joinery." The kintsugi method conveys a philosophy not of replacement, but of awe, reverence, and restoration. The gold-filled cracks of a once-broken item are a testament to its history.

It does not take a great leap of thought to apply this to ourselves. As we live through experiences which challenge and threaten to destroy us, how are we when we emerge? I recently came across an interesting article by a Scottish woman, living and working in Asia as a humanitarian and development professional who uses the pseudonym "Feisty Blue Gecko—A tail of the unexpected." She describes how she had just taken up a new post in Myanmar when she was diagnosed with Stage 3 Breast Cancer late in 2009. In relating to the Kintsukuroi art, she says that "the instant that the bowl drops and smashes, is just like that moment when you hear those unforgettable words and learn that you have cancer. Everything which is precious and sure, suddenly shatters and it feels impossible that it could ever be mended. The hideous different types of treatment continue to break the bowl into smaller fragments. But as we struggle physically, there is a gold thread which emerges with gradual repair." She relates in her articles on breast cancer awareness that the broken pieces are many because of the damage inflicted on her body from the immediate treatments and from continued medication. She narrates how she feels aggrieved by that which has been damaged or stolen by cancer. The constrained mobility thanks to joint pain, weight gain despite regular exercise, reduced energy, lungs which have been damaged by the embolism, and blood levels which require regular monitoring to ensure that she is in a "safe zone." In spite of all this she goes on to say that "Yet there is a less tangible element. This gold thread is one of resilience, inner determination, the will and need to focus on that which is important."

Many of us may have experienced in life some level of pain, abuse or degree of ill-treatment which shook us, broke us and possibly threatened our identity and wholeness. It is important to realise that we can cross over to yet another dimension of wholeness as we allow our spirit to grow in the knowledge of the Creator who created mankind in His own image according to Genesis 1:26-27.

THE TRAUMA OF ABUSE

Located 146 km south of Harare on the main road south to Masvingo and South Africa, Chivhu (formerly Enkeldoorn) is a small town in Zimbabwe. Chivhu historically has an agricultural economy, based in poultry farming and dairy cattle. In this small town lies Mtoro, a ward sparsely populated by black medium scale farmers who purchased sizeable pieces of land prior to the Zimbabwe independence period. Owing to the rich pasture land, good farming soils and favourable climate, this area was a vibrant hive of activity which attracted diligent and hardworking farm labourers from different towns in Zimbabwe. In the Rhodesian era, the farm which my father bought as an investment was one of the most well renowned pieces of land boasting of a beautiful landscape with several streams on undulating slopes, an abattoir, a dam, thick vegetation a General dealer store with well-maintained infrastructure to support cattle ranching and farming activities.

Growing up as a young girl on the farm, rural life at the farm did not offer any special privileges especially for my unfortunate situation at that time. Routine tasks of farm work ensued daily under the direct supervision of my elders who were my primary care givers and the hired general hand who was from a foreign land. On the occasions that my younger relatives from Harare joined us at the farm at the end of the school term, it was always a welcome relief to have companionship and extra help with the tough rural life. Daily homestead routine tasks included rising early before dawn to release the flocks from their paddocks into the pastures and then resuming with water fetching duties before getting on with the seasonal farming tasks such as ploughing, weeding or harvesting grains from the vast acres of land. Age and gender at a farm do not attract any special privileges. If anything, the women folk tend to do more than their male counterparts. Such was the life that greeted me when I came into this world in the late Rhodesia era. As the elders went about their daily routine farm tasks there was none to lend pity to this fragile young life that lived a life of solitude amongst the great company of bleating sheep, stubborn goats and strong willed oxen. The elders in my day had no time for frivolous complaints and anything that could have been easily perceived as laziness. The first time that I gathered the courage to tell one of my elders about the violent sexual abuses I was suffering regularly at the hands of the farm worker as I herded the flocks, she quickly dismissed me with threats of beatings and more. Knowing that there was no shield and rescue, these forced encounters continued unabated every time as we went about our daily tasks milking the cows, shepherding the flocks to different paddocks, drinking pans or pastures, fetching firewood in the forest or even at the homestead. No amount of screaming could alert anyone or bring rescue as the buildings and farms were far part from each other and there were thickets of tall grass and forests. At such a tender age I could never understand what pleasure a grown middle aged man could possibly derive from forcing himself on an innocent and tender young girl, too young to be in school and still continue this for years to come without any remorse or fear of being caught. He never did get caught or reprimanded and he continued to work at the farm for several years afterwards. All I remembered over the years from the encounters were the putrid odours and helplessness that comes with any innocent creature being ravished by a heartless devouring rapist. The few times that I would be sent to spend the day assisting at the General Dealer store I would allow my mind to wander away to lands yonder as I would watch folks bustling to buy refreshments as they alighted from the Chigumba AVM bus that faithfully serviced the Harare-Chivhu-Mtoro-Sadza route during that era. The hurried revving of the engine by the driver would make my heart race with excitement as though I was one of the passengers. I filled my mind with fantasies of life in Harare, escaping the emotional and psychological prison that had engulfed my world at such a tender age. With a loud threating horn the driver would rev more ferociously as the bus conductor made final rounds calling out to all the passengers in the store to return to the bus whilst securing on the top carrier loads of luggage for the new passengers boarding from the station at the store. The passengers would excitedly bustle back into the bus and I would look longingly at their cold, shapely bottles of Tarino soft drinks and fresh candy cakes topped with delicious pink icing on top. I contrasted this with the regular servings of *"Sadza nemunyevhe" (Sadza with* African spider flower leaves) which we would harvest freshly in abundance from the cattle kraal where it grew in abundance because of the fertile dung soils. This was alternated once in a while with the special delicacy of *"Sadza nehodzeko"* (Sadza with cultured milk) specially prepared by my grandmother. We only had mouthfuls of this delicacy when there were no visitors otherwise the children would have to scrounge around the *"mutuvi"* (cultured milk fermented extracts). As the bus drove away raising dust in the clean rural air, the sound of the engine would begin to fade away in the far distance and so would my excitement as I returned to the reality of the broken life I had. In the stillness of the night as my mind raced and as I tossed and turned in my bed I could still hear Chigumba droning in the distance. In my mind's eye I could see it spitting gusts of dust as it drove away from the Chirinda General Dealer store in Mtoro headed for Harare, the town of nights, renowned for her people who do not sleep. It felt as if the dust was laughing in my face and preparing to bury me in the dark misery of life in rural Chivhu.

From Brokenness to Confidence

Decades later having been blessed with a wonderful family, and by the saving grace of a loving God the trauma has dissipated. At the back of my mind I shudder to think how many young girls in different parts of the world face such brutality and violent ordeals with no one to protect them or shield them from such shattering experiences. The testimony of the power in the blood of Jesus which is able to heal all and restore full life has faithfully remained my beacon of strength and courage knowing that in spite of everything the enemy had designed for my destruction, God has taken every piece and beautifully fortified it with His unique craft to be used as a vessel to minister to other broken lives and exhort them to a place of confidence in the Lord. Even after having gone through this pain in my early childhood, the progression life brings with it countless curve balls. I have had to navigate through all of them standing on a solid and firm foundation of faith in order to overcome and come out strong. It is important to know that life is not about waiting for the storms to end, but learning to dance in the rain! As you put your total trust in God through the pain you will come out stronger and fortified with godly confidence. Confidence is not something that can be learned like a set of rules; confidence is a state of mind. Positive thinking, prophetic faith affirmations, practice, training, knowledge and talking to other people are all useful ways to help improve broken individuals to increase their confidence levels. More than anything it is important for individuals who have gone through painful violation to forgive themselves and accept that there is a new covenant of grace that brings restoration and glistening beauty in that place of brokenness in spite of the cause of their brokenness. Confidence comes from feelings of well-being, acceptance of your body and mind (self-esteem) and belief in what God has created you to be.

THE ORDINANCE OF COMMUNION

The ordinance of Communion is something most Christians celebrate on a regular basis during their church services. It's commonly referred to as "The Lord's Table." And on that "table" are two elements—emblems that represent two very important aspects of Christianity. Those two elements are the cup and the bread. The cup represents the blood of Jesus that was shed on the Cross for the remission of our sin. The bread represents the body of Jesus that was broken for us. Jesus came to earth and announced, "I am the living bread that came down from Heaven" John 6:51 (NIV). Through Christ Jesus, a whole new dimension of living has been made available to us. When we accept Jesus Christ into our heart and life, partaking by faith in His broken body and shed blood, we walk into a new dimension of life.

Natural bread is earthly, but spiritual bread is heavenly. Natural bread is corruptible, but spiritual bread is incorruptible. Natural bread is limited, but spiritual bread is unlimited. Natural bread feeds the body; spiritual bread feeds the spirit. We need to realize that without the shedding of blood, there is no remission of sin. It is very important that we recognize what the cup and the blood represents. We need to give the bread the recognition that it needs. It represents the Living Bread Who walked upon the earth and was sacrificed for our wholeness and soundness of body.

The bread represents our Lord. He walked this earth in a physical body. In that body, He taught along the seashore. He sailed the Sea of Galilee. He went about doing good and healing all who were oppressed of the devil (Acts 10:38). And that body was broken for me and you. That body was lashed with thirty-nine stripes—by whose stripes we were healed (1 Peter 2:24)! That body was hung on the cross, buried in a grave, and raised again! That body is the Living Bread! Our Lord is the Bread of Life! How do we partake of the Living Bread? We do it by faith. When we partake of the Communion wafer (a natural bread), we eat it and acknowledge by faith that we are partaking of spiritual bread, the Bread of Life. The natural bread is a representation of the spiritual bread. Partaking of the bread is a natural act with spiritual meaning and significance. By faith, we remember what Jesus did for us. By faith, we partake of Christ's broken body and shed blood. By faith, we celebrate the healing and salvation Christ has provided.

In his book, *Christ: The Bread of Life*, Kenneth W. Hagin Jr encourages that every time you take Communion, you ought to release your faith and receive all that the Communion table represents. Bodily healing, psychological healing, emotional healing, together with eternal salvation are offered at the Communion table of blessing. Healing and a brand-new dimension of life belong to you. The next time you partake of the Lord's Table, determine in your heart to receive all that the Lord has provided for you!

CONTEMPLATIVE MOMENTS:
READ THROUGH AND REFLECT BEFORE THE ACTION

Are you battling with an inferiority complex today? Are you nursing something that is broken in your life? Are the pieces coming together? Have you prayerfully sought for your healing in that place of brokenness? What and who have you allowed to look down on you? Forgive yourself, release your failures and embrace fresh confidence in your new identity in Christ. Remember that confidence is a state of mind—it comes from your feelings of well-being as you accept who God has beautifully created you to be!

My commitments for this week: I COMMIT to _____
_____
_____

My affirmations: I AM _____
_____
_____

My transformative actions this month: I WILL _____
(1) _____
(2) _____
(3) _____

Chapter Five

Refuelling from Emptiness

In life as we pursue the deep sense of belonging, we can easily become engulfed by the overpowering desire to be found in the company of others as we shun our own company. Social connections are beautiful, warm and often comforting. When we are in the pleasurable company of our family, friends, acquaintances and colleagues, we become engaged in other matters and dialogues that often take us away from the present realities in our own lives. Social connections are necessary for our vitality. Nevertheless, our personal development is threatened when our over-indulgence in social company takes over the precious moments that we ought to invest in times of reflection, reviewing and planning ahead. Dialogues are powerful, they help us to appreciate different opinions and worldviews. They sometimes entertain us and help us to forget our worries. Dialogues become ruinous when they overtake the critical internal voices that monologues bring. Meaningful monologues are very difficult to engage in when we are constantly in dialogue. What kind of emotions do you experience when you are alone? Do you feel bored? Do you feel unhappy? Do you feel miserable and fearful?

THE PAIN OF REJECTION

Rejection wounds hurt deeply because rejection attacks the very person that we are. It destroys our self-esteem, our self-value, self-worth and our purpose in life. This is why it is one of the most common tools the devil will use to destroy a person's life. God never wanted us to feel rejected or abandoned. He desires for you to know who you really are, and realize how deeply God loves, accepts, and appreciates you, so that you can live out the fullness of what all God has ordained you to be. God's Word tells us that without being rooted and grounded in the love (and acceptance) of God, we cannot experience the fullness of God in our lives: "And to know the love of Christ, which passeth knowledge, that ye might be filled with all the fullness of God. (Ephesians 3:19)

Rejection has a way of destroying a person's life in a way that few other things can. The sad fact is that the number of people who are affected by rejection is staggering. If we want to be all that God has created us to be, then overcoming rejection and its effects is vital and absolutely essential. Whether you have experienced rejection from the womb, from childhood, in a dating relationship or marriage, the wound of rejection creates a doorway for demonic activities in your life which need to be addressed and closed for you to find wholeness. The wounds of rejection can open a person up to many other unclean spirits which will then require those who have ongoing struggles to undergo deliverance ministration as led by the power of the Holy Spirit in order to have those spirits removed. Rejection can result in performance orientation, rebellion, violence, self-harm, sexual promiscuity, sexual perversion and other extreme behaviours. Lack of love as a child, for example, can cause that child to turn to pornography and lust to fulfill their need to be loved.

THE DYNAMICS OF REJECTION

The closer a person is to you, the deeper their rejection can wound you. Authority figures are also able to deeply wound you, because you look up to them and rely upon them. Whether you love or hate a person doesn't make anybody immune from rejection. You can literally want to kill somebody, but still be affected by their rejection. The question is, are you looking to them for approval? Are you basing your identity upon what they think of you? Does their approval of you give your life meaning and purpose?

A person's age also has a lot to do with their vulnerability to rejection. Children are especially vulnerable to the damage of rejection, because they are still developing their identity and learning about who they are. A lot of damage is done by peers in school. Either you are too short, too tall, too fat, too skinny, you have brown eyes when you should have blue eyes... you name it, and kids will pick on it! Insecure children can be very cruel and damage other children through rejection. Why? Because their own identity is not based on the right things. They do not know who they really are, or who they are called to be, so they go around putting other kids down to make themselves feel better.

Dealing with Rejection

You cannot settle rejection issues fully until you get it down into your spirit that you are accepted, loved, and appreciated by God. Dealing with religious strongholds is vital to this process, as religion paints God as distant, cold, and impersonal. Bringing your relationship with God into proper perspective is a vital step in the process of overcoming the strongholds of rejection. Tearing down the strongholds of rejection is as simple as merely receiving, with childlike faith, what God's Word has to say about your identity, who you are as a new creature in Christ, who is called to life, purpose, and meaning in Christ. The one thing that you absolutely cannot overlook is correcting your identity. You need to start seeing yourself for who you are in Christ, and the person that God has really formed within you. Your identity must come from Him and what His Word says about you. Forgiving those who have rejected you is a starting point, even when they have not approached you to ask for forgiveness and even when they fail to acknowledge the pain they have caused you.

The Power of Solitude

As human beings, we are social creatures and, without others around us from birth, we would not even be able to stay alive in this world. Social space plays a crucial role in the development of our personality, as the direction of our development is determined by the expectations of other people and our desire to meet those expectations. We enjoy the company of other people and the activities that allows us to connect to people. If you feel miserable and unhappy when you are alone then you may lack the power of solitude. The power of solitude is the expression that is used to describe the trait that allows a person to feel good and adequate when they are alone. What makes a person unable to stay alone is their external dependency which is the desire to escape from their bad mood by doing anything that could keep them occupied. The more miserable you feel in your own company, the more likely you are going to be dependent on someone else to escape from your negative emotions and avoid facing your problems. Escaping to social life when you have big problems is not bad in itself provided that you work on a solution instead of ignoring the problem. People who escape from their problems and never try to solve them end up depressed. Creativity flourishes in solitude. It allows you to dive into ideas, focus on problems, think outside the box, and reach deep within yourself and your imagination in a way that is not possible around others.

WHERE CAN YOU BE ADDRESSED?

As human beings we exist simultaneously on many levels (body-soul-spirit), which are interconnected and synergistic. Henri Nouwen, in his book Making All things New says that "one way to express the spiritual crisis of our time is to say that most of us have an address but cannot be found there. We know where we belong, but we keep being pulled away in many directions, as if we were still homeless. 'All these other things' keep demanding our attention. They lead us so far from home that we eventually forget our true address, that is, the place where we can be addressed." Clearly, social wellness is an integral part of overall health. As with anything, however, social well-being is about balance more than absolutes. We need others because we have many unmet needs. The more unmet needs we have the needier we will be when it comes to spending time with others. If you constantly need reassurance or attention then you might find yourself unable to stay alone even for few hours.

What is Shaping our Hearts and Minds?

Our modern culture brings with it more complications. We are often impelled by the technological imperative to stay connected. People take laptops on vacation, their smart phones to bed with them. With the constant access to virtual if not actual socialization, experts wonder if we have forgotten how to be completely alone, wholly cut off for a time. Can we truly submerge ourselves in solitude when we're fighting the urge to check email or our social network updates "one more time"? It is no secret that we are bombarded everyday with countless messages. The advertising industry gladly spends billions of dollars into communications because they know that over time, they will shape our minds, hearts, and spending habits. All of these messages inevitably begin to shape our lives. Our heart and mind is indeed influenced by the messages that enter through our eyes and ears. And our life is slowly whittled away and re-formed by the loudest voices that get through. Being alone allows you to be with your own thoughts and discover your own voice. It is in these moments of solitude where you discover your true identity and means of expression. You are free from any interruptions or outside opinions. It is just your own voice.

How Do You Use Your Alone Time?

The power of being alone should not be dismissed. Unfortunately, our culture has transformed the idea of being alone into some sort of eccentricity that the well-adjusted individual should not experience. In this case, we are talking about being alone and not being lonely, although it seems the distinction has been blurred. Solitude has much to offer in all facets of our lives and a conscious effort should be made by every individual to experience it regularly. Four quadrants to consider in life are Alone time, People Time, Work Time and Play Time. Alone Time allows for reflection and defusing. This time enables one to unwind and evaluate. We need to use alone time to process our relationships and recalibrate our sense of self.

Solitude provides opportunities to rediscover our lives. By electing to intentionally withdraw from human relationships for a period of time, we are able to remove the shaping influence of others and "re-centre" our hearts on our deepest values. Often times, we realize that these shaping forces have been incorrect all along and we have lost our lives because of them. When we embrace solitude we intentionally remove the influence of others for period of time. We intentionally remove the expectations of others and are able to hear our own heart speak. In solitude we find rest and refreshment, we also discover that others can live without us. Moments of solitude help us to adequately reflect on our past and chart our future. We break the cycle of busyness in our lives. We become better equipped to show patience with others and we feed our souls.

Take time to listen: Staying on Course with Your Life Mission

The myriad sweet melodies of birds mingling with the novelty of every naive morning would fill our ears before they were drowned by the bellowing sound of cows donning cow-bells and transporting noisy metal carts around our industrious community in rural Chivhu. The birds' harmonious tunes heralded the start of a new day and sounded like a well-choreographed musical piece as they gently received swishing and rustling applauses from the tree branches yawning in adoration of the new day in anticipation of the bright and warm sun rays. Such was the signature of my childhood mornings in the beloved rural birth-land of Chivhu. Singing with one accord yet in so many different tunes one could almost tell what the weather would bring that day depending on which bird sang loudest and in the intensity of the tunes. The popular bird we used to mimic as *"mugovera muchaparara"* (destruction on Saturday) would often herald a day filled with much hustle and bustle in the sweltering heat of a rural day according to the interpretation of our elders then.

During one windy August when our cousin from Harare came to visit during the school holidays she was stunned that all our movements as rural folk seemed to be so well synchronised as though in response to some invisible clock as she found everyone shuffling in the dark and beginning to get ready for the day without anyone rousing the other from the night slumber. On the third day witnessing this early morning routine she asked me how we knew that is was time to get up and go about when it was still so dark and the cock had not even crowed. I then explained to her that once one stays in a familiar environment for a while they developed an acquired sensitivity to sound, rhythms and tunes from the outside world which registered internally without the need for a clock and alarm. It was this embedded and acquired sensitivity that the rural folk would use to guide them in understanding the season and hour of day and even to know whether it would rain on that day before observing the clouds. Whilst the birds in the forest seemed to make one choral outfit, over time one would acquire a skill for discerning which bird was singing and what that it foretold. It is this ability to discern that helped us from a young age to stay in tune with the external environment without any schooling on geography's time and weather patterns. By the time she left us to go back to Harare she had only managed to learn the names of some of the birds and mimic some of their sounds when we took her around the forests but could barely discern when more than two bird genres belted out their melodious harmonies all at once.

Taking time to listen is a skill that one acquires when they allow themselves to search out the quiet sound and inner voices. Whilst the calls and songs of birds travel better in more serene environments, the fact remains that wherever birds reside they will continue to call to each other or sing for different reasons in different seasons. The onus is on the avid and sensitive listener to hear the sound and unique voice when it is released. In much the same way every new day heralds the release of a myriad of voices into the atmosphere of this world. The voices you hear are determined by your listening skills, level of sensitivity and preparedness to shut out everything else and discern the voices. The myriad of voices released vary from one's own voice, the spiritual voice and the voices in the surrounding world.

The latter often tends to drown one's own inner voice and their spiritual voice if one is not given to the discipline of taking time to listen.

So why bother to take time and listen in a world where information and knowledge is awash and available at the touch of a button? The question is whether you can discern the right voice for you for every moment of your day. Discernment of voices is a vital skill which everyone ought to yearn for because it is from these inner voices that we gain insight, wisdom, guidance and direction for the decisions that we need to make in every waking moment, whether simple or complex. It is important to know when to listen to which voice so that we do not lose track of our destiny, mission and life assignments.

We often do not take time to listen because everything in this age is happening so fast and we fear that any moment lost in discerning thoughts, voices and messages may cost us opportunities as the world flies by so fast. We neglect to think though of how severely wrong opportunities and decisions may punish us in the long term if they are rushed into and not carefully considered. Often we are too busy or pre-occupied with dialogue and caught up in information overload via flooding mass communications from every direction to the extent that we lose focus on our authentic centre and inner voice. In the same way that the many varieties of birds belt out a variety of tunes at the same time so are there many voices being released into this world every day of our lives. The question is which voice should we listen to? The voices we catch are determined by the moments of solitude we allow for ourselves as well as the frequencies that we tune into throughout the day. We need to develop a relationship with the vital voices in our lives if we are to remain on our destined track to avoid becoming impulsive in our behaviour. It is the wavelength that you ride on that determines the frequency you tune into. Sometimes our frequencies are determined and regulated by the company we keep and even more sadly by ourselves when we shut down the vital inner voices which we ought to pay attention to. Without a relationship with these vital voices, the important signals will always be weaker in comparison to the dominant noises that prevail and bombard our world and thoughts. Determine to position yourself in the correct frequency today as you take time out to listen out for the still voices which are ready to give you wisdom, guidance and direction as you make decisions and discern the changing seasons and times.

CULTIVATE WHOLESOME SPEECH

Growing up in the deep rural leafy farming lands, I remember vividly how our elders always hushed us up with some air of mysticism when we walked through the forests as we gathered firewood or when we crossed the rivers walking through dark paths in the evening. They would always chide us for our loudness and endless chatter reminding us to honour and respect the unseen powers that resided in the forests and darkness that had power to steal our words and voices. Enveloped in childhood innocence and my natural African expressive nature I could never wrap my little mind around the cause for this constant rebuke. The instances that we defied this order to observe silence both my cousin and I received unforgettable pull-and-twist ear pinches ever so harshly that we would savour the vibrating heat and temporary deafness which lasted for what seemed like eternity. That managed to keep us silent for a while. When we arrived home we would be told stories of how people were made to disappear in the deep darkness for saying things that offended "those in the forests and the air" and how others lost their voices forever or lost their minds from foolish chatter. They would often remind us of Boreman the "village madman" who had lost his mind completely because he insulted the unseen in his drunken stupor one day as he walked home from a drinking spree. What I could never understand was why the adults were allowed to continue with their conversations even though it was either in hushed tones or deep guttural tones, yet we were condemned to uphold total silence, a very hard sentence for the expressive bolts of energy that we were.

As years went by I began to realise that the grace to speak seemed to be easily granted us by the elders as we were now deemed to be "more responsible with our words." Decades later I realise now that the expectation for responsible speech is placed on every mature adult who should be held accountable for the outcome of their words. It was later explained to us that the "silence sentence" was enforced on the children because they tend to be reckless with their speech and are not given to wise, discerning and appropriate words as occasion demands. Whilst the mystery of "the hidden powers in the dark" is still upheld and reverenced in different perceptions depending on culture and religious belief, I do realise now that the intangible atmosphere that surrounds us is not as simple as it may appear but holds in it the power to work with the spoken words that proceed from our mouths. With more exposure and deeper understanding of how the tangible world interacts with the intangible or unseen realm I now appreciate the power that words released can yield.

Sometimes our upbringing and backgrounds lend us habitually to vile speech which becomes second nature because we have a misinformed concept of "freedom of speech." A wholesome tongue comes from a transformed mindset that embraces wholesome thinking which is considerate, sensitive and progressive. Wholesome speech yields in it the power to build and produce vitality and fruitful living for individuals, families, communities and nations. Unwholesome speech does not only refer to vulgarities and obscenities but poorly processed words that become can become daggers to the hearers. Some of the ravaging wars that have scarred the African continent regrettably come from speech that is not wholesome and the results are evidently destructive. Speech once it is released has the power to execute a creative or destructive mandate even when it was unintended because words cannot be taken back in the true sense of the expression. Corrupt speech if often characterised by underlying bitterness, anger and malice which have the potential to ruin healthy relationships, distance those who love us and destroy wholesome living. Very often we do not take time to self-introspect and analyse our speech and sometimes it is the quality of the company we surround ourselves with that can diminish or groom our speech.

It is incumbent upon all of us to conduct a regular self-analysis of how the lives we are living could be as a result of the words that we release daily into the atmosphere of our homes and beyond which can either release blessing or come back as a deadly boomerang to haunt us and our posterity. Our speech is a verbal expression of our thoughts. What is your speech building and attracting to your life?

CONTEMPLATIVE MOMENTS:
READ THROUGH AND REFLECT BEFORE THE ACTION

Are you able to identify the things that drain you and leave you with a feeling of emptiness inside? Are you doing anything to address those energy and emotional drainers? Have you ever suffered from rejection in your life? Do you feel that you have dealt with it from the root? How much alone time do you give yourself in a day or a week? What voices are you listening to and which frequencies are you tuned into? What could be distracting you from listening to the vital voices in your life? How wholesome is your self-talk?

My commitments for this week: I COMMIT to _____
_____
_____

My affirmations: I AM _____
_____
_____

My transformative actions this month: I WILL _____
(1) _____
(2) _____
(3) _____

Chapter Six

Refreshing Waters

Mvura naya naya, tidye mupunga / zulu zulu buya sihle amakhomane!

Thomas Fuller once said, "We never know the worth of water till the well is dry." After weeks and months of agony in the historical heat wave that hit Zimbabwe and the surrounding region towards the end of 2015, the heavy rains that started falling midway into the first quarter of 2016 brought a sense of relief to many even though hopes for reviving crops at that stage had all died away. Many whose crops and livestock had died in the heat and drought season almost cursed the rains for coming so late when there was nothing remaining to salvage. In spite of all that, when the pain and disappointment is washed away, the people still rejoice at the coming of the water because of the hope for a life beyond the heat and the loss. Kariba dam hit a historical all time low and this made the people panic. Some weeks later, the raindrops pounded heavily on the earth which was waiting readily for it after what seemed an endlessly eternity of being scorched by the merciless sun. It is on a day like this that children can sing loudly *"mvura naya naya tidye mupunga/ zulu zulu buya sihle amakhoman*e." At the onset of the rain season a frequent sight is of children holding hands and dancing round and round in a circle as they look up expectantly into the sky, singing this rhyme as they encourage the rains to descend so that they can harvest and eat rice. In Zimbabwe the rice crop in grown in a muddy field.

The Life in the Water

From the beginning water has sustained lives. Human cultures have flourished due to the availability of water for drinking and for cultivation. Great rivers such as the Nile, Niger, Limpopo and Zambezi gave birth to African civilizations. Water is so essential to life in Southern Africa that the people of Botswana use the greeting Pula, meaning rain, a term also used for their currency. Today water still dominates our lives and its presence continues to govern the location of homes and cities; its availability or lack of it can cause deaths among people, animals and plants. Water shortages can cause conflict between individuals, communities, countries and regions. The irony is that water is also nurturing, linking communities hundreds of kilometres apart, by lakes and rivers, and fostering kinship and trade relations. While water in the form of rain may bring joy to farmers because it foretells the promise of a good planting and growing season, as well as harvest, it has also brought disaster in many parts of the world through floods, which have killed thousands of people and left many others homeless. Such tragedies occur frequently in many parts of the world.

Water plays an important role in different cultures and societies. In the Mutoko district in Zimbabwe, visitors are welcomed to a homestead with a glass of water to drink. In many parts of Zimbabwe a new bride collects water for members of the family of her in-laws household and heats the water for each of their bath. This traditional ceremony is done as a welcome gesture into the family for the bride as well as a means of cementing her relationship with her new family. Traditional and religious herbalists are known to use water to cleanse a person who is possessed by evil spirits. In many cases the person is instructed to bathe in swiftly running water or to stand under a waterfall. White garment priests give bottled water to people suffering from different ailments after fasting and praying for the water to attain healing powers. When one is converted to Christianity one receives water baptism to fulfill one's conversion. Christians believe that when one is immersed in baptism water the old sinful self is drowned and buried in the water while the new repentant person emerges out of the water.

Water played a significant role in Biblical times. The entire earth was destroyed by water except for faithful Noah together with his family members and a host of animals. Naaman was healed of leprosy when he dipped himself seven times in the river Jordan. The Israelites escaped from Pharoah's wrath by crossing a parted Red Sea and Pharoah's soldiers were drowned to their destruction by the same waters when they marched on after the safe passage of the Israelites. Jesus Christ walked on the water, much to the amazement of His disciples and He also calmed a raging sea of water. (Extracts taken from Memory Dete's *"Let it rain, may blessings come,"* (November 5, 2008))

God Wants to Brings Us to A Good Land

As in the story of the children of Israel, God's intention is to bring us all the way into the full enjoyment of the all-inclusive Christ as the reality of the good land. However, God is not negligent of the means and the process through which He takes care of us and brings us into the good land. In all our Christian journey "in the wilderness" today God wants to be our provision, the fountain of living waters for us to drink and enjoy to be satisfied and supplied. God's intention in His economy is to be the fountain of living waters to us so that we as His people may be satisfied with Him for our enjoyment and become the church as God's increase, God's enlargement, to be God's fullness for His expression. Jeremiah 2:13 is a verse that exposes us all: we may not do many bad or evil things, but we may forsake God as the source of living waters and "hew out" cisterns for ourselves, cisterns which are broken and hold no water.

Nothing in this world can quench our thirst or really satisfy us; nothing but the Triune God in Christ as the Spirit flowing into us as living waters can satisfy us and quench our thirst. This is why the Lord Jesus, at the end of the feast, stood out and cried, "If any man thirst, let him come to Me and drink!" (John 7:37-39). The Lord became the Spirit who now is the flowing river of water of life: we simply need to come to Him and drink! God's intention is not for us to do material things for Him but to come to Him and take Him in so that He may work Himself into our being and flow into us and out of us for the fulfillment of His eternal purpose.

In Exodus 17:6, right at the beginning of their journey through the wilderness, the children of Israel were at the foothill of Mount Horeb, and they had no water. It is vitally important in the wilderness to have water: if there's no water, it is impossible to survive. The Bedouins live "from water to water", from one source of water to another; if you don't find water while travelling through the wilderness, you die. When the people saw they had no water, they contended with Moses, asking him to give them water, and then they tested Jehovah saying, "Is Jehovah with us or not? How come we got into this situation?" However, the Lord did not rebuke His people; rather, He stood upon the rock and asked Moses to strike the rock so that water may flow out for people to drink. This all happened in the beginning of their journey through the wilderness. Later, toward the end of their journey, when they were close to Canaan, they ran out of water again in Numbers chapter 20; again, they murmured against Moses and cried out to the Lord, and instead of rebuking them, God provided water for them.

This is such a clear picture of our Christian life: in our Christian life we are travelling through the wilderness, and we should not have any bitterness as happened at Marah in the wilderness. Nevertheless, throughout our Christian life we come to times when there is dryness. We come to situations where there's no water and we are really thirsty. Dryness cannot always be avoided in our Christian life. Sometimes due to circumstances in our family life, our health, or our spiritual situation, we enter into a period of dryness. We should not consider this as being strange; we can avoid temptation and murmuring, as God allows dryness and temptation to test us and cause us to grow in life (1 Corinthians 10:13). We should not consider the fiery ordeals coming upon us as something strange; they are part of the Christian walk, and in the midst of all these situations, God is faithful. God is faithful to bring us into the fellowship of His Son that we may enjoy Him and partake of Him (1 Corinthians. 1:30). In the same way, God is faithful even when we are tempted or when we are dry. He will not bring us into a situation that is beyond what we are able to bear; rather, He will make a way of escape for us! He may not bring us out of our financial crisis or family problem but He wants us to drink the water of life so that we may have the grace to endure it.

Are You Ready for the Rain?

Rain Rain go away,
Come again another day.
Little children want to play...

"Rain Rain Go Away" is a popular English language nursery rhyme which has been modified to various versions. Sometimes when the rain eventually comes in our lives we are not always prepared for it and we may even feel that it is disrupting our routine activities. I remember that as we were growing up we were taught that if we wanted the rain to go away we needed to throw grains of salt around the homestead. We believed that this would chase away the rain when we wanted to either play, work or needing the grains to dry in the sun or for the clothes to dry on the laundry line.

You may never have the perfect weather conditions that suit your fancy all the time. Regardless of your age or the weather conditions in whichever part of the world you may be, what is most important is to make a determined effort to create your own atmosphere within and around you. If you continually allow the external weather elements to determine your mood and your outlook on life you are bound to lose so many years waiting for the perfect conditions for you to unleash your potential or manifest in your areas of giftedness. Do not become bitter because of the wilderness experiences but allow yourself to be refreshed and restored by God's healing waters. Proverbs 19: tells us that. You can activate the words of your mouth to be like healing water by filling them with godly wholesomeness as you prophesy into your own life. John 7:38 says that "He that believeth on me, as the scripture hath said, out of his belly shall flow rivers of living water." We are also reminded in Proverbs 18:20 that "A man's belly shall be satisfied with the fruit of his mouth; and with the increase of his lips shall he be filled."

CONTEMPLATIVE MOMENTS:
READ THROUGH AND REFLECT BEFORE THE ACTION

Have you walked through a wilderness that left you dry and parched in so many areas of your life? What have you done to refresh and replenish those areas? Do you have any bitterness because of the things that you have gone through? What will it take you to forgive and allow fresh water to wash through your pain? Who can help you to go through this?

My commitments for this week: I COMMIT to _____
_____
_____

My affirmations: I AM _____
_____
_____

My transformative actions this month: I WILL _____
(1) _____
(2) _____
(3) _____

Chapter Seven:

The Perfect Finish – From Success to Significance

One of my most vivid childhood memories of growing up surrounded by the lovely green foliage of rural Zimbabwe, is found in the smell of sweaty blistered hands from hard work in the long unending furrows of farming land. When it came to work in the fields there were no excuses accepted in respect of age, gender or state of health. I can still hear the regular reprimands from the elders whenever fatigue started to settle in my tiny arms and an overseeing voice would suddenly roar *"vasikana muri kumanza, simbisai maoko ayo mubate badza iro"* (you are leaving weeds in the field, get a proper grip of the hoe and do a thorough job). If ever there was a time I learnt the power of self-talk and positive confession, this was it. Those were the joys of rural life. By the time you took a breather to take a sip of *mahewu* (traditionally brewed African beverage), your hands will have a familiar quiver and shake as you took hold of the gourd filled with the sweet liquid. The common mantra from our elders in that era was that "the lazy one should not eat," so hard work was the order of the day.

In life, anything that you want to achieve is going to take time and, most importantly, effort. Time is our most valuable asset and if we are truly invested in something, our efforts and time will be all we have to offer. Nothing comes easy in this world and if we really want something, then we are going to stop at nothing to make it happen. Finding your passion may be the most difficult part of your life, but once you find it, you will stop at nothing to make your dreams come true. In life, like in business, you have the people who are out there living it to the fullest and the bystanders letting it pass them by. You have the people who sit around and mope all day about how miserable their lives are, then you have the people who are out there crossing things off their bucket lists on a regular basis. In business, you have the people who started from nothing and didn't do anything to change their situations, then you have the people who saw whatever little opportunity they had and made the most of it.

AMBITIONS OF FAME

I still have very vivid memories when we were growing up in Harare (Zimbabwe's capital city) in the early 80s, my school mates would hysterically go wild with excitement when they received post card responses from the Michael Jackson fan club. None of them would ever accept to believe that these beautifully penned, personalised responses were being generated by the fan club employees and not the celebrity himself. Vicious words would often be exchanged as the young ladies fought over who had received a more personalised and affectionate response from the music icon who had stolen the hearts of many through his music fame, wealth and endearing looks. I shall not mention here how many girls feigned to be talented musicians in destitute situations in Africa desperately needing to be "rescued" by an air ticket to the "dreamland of America." Waiting anxiously for the Postman during that era of snail mail became a precious pastime. The young people became so consumed by Michael's worldwide fame and huge success in the music industry. Both the young men and women were not only obsessed by his personality and success but devoted hours and days in the precious art of mimicking the famous star. I can still picture them purring away that "they would like to be famous like Michael Jackson and make lots of money" whenever they were asked about their aspirations and life ambitions. This goal possessed their very being and their convictions made them believe that their best end ever would only be realised when they were rich and famous in the "dreamland" overseas.

What is the Psychology of Fame and Power?

How and why do people change when they become famous or powerful? The psychology of fame is different for each person who experiences it, but there are some common threads. A study which interviewed a number of people who had achieved fame tried to break down the psychological phases and consequences of fame. Most of them remarked how at first fame feels good, yet something about it does not feel quite right. "The lure of adoration is attractive, and it becomes difficult for the person to imagine living without fame." One participant said, 'I've been addicted to almost every substance known to man at one point or another, and the most addicting of them all is fame.'" At first, the experience of becoming famous provides much ego stroking. Newly famous people find themselves warmly embraced. There is a guilty pleasure associated with the thrill of being admired in that participants both love the attention and adoration while they question the gratification they experience from fame. Some experience a loss of self, and a conflict between self and their public persona. "Living up to others' expectations becomes a vicious cycle, in which the celebrity, like a hamster on a wheel, works to satisfy a hungry and demanding public."

In Greed of the Glory

Fame brings out some ugly beasts that, if not tamed, can consume a person's life. One taste of the spotlight and greed feeds the desire for more. The adoration is gratifying until the high wears off. Fame is enticing. Who does not want to jet-set around the globe with a limitless budget? That would be our version of heaven on earth, would it not? To have it all - popularity, money, adoring fans worshiping our every move. The problem with this type of lifestyle is that the exhilaration eventually disappears. Stardom is the great deceiver that blinds people into thinking more money or power or prestige will solve their problems. Robin Williams inspired an entire generation of movie buffs and actors when they were just children. But his tragic end in an apparent suicide has also served notice of the dangers that come with fame. Williams struggled for years with substance abuse and depression, and his death came just months after that of another huge Hollywood star, actor Philip Seymour Hoffman, who died of a heroin overdose as he relapsed after years being clean. Dr Tom Nunan, founder of Bull's Eye Entertainment and a professor at the UCLA School of Theatre, Film and Television, said Williams' career showed young actors that "they really can do anything. They can perform on Broadway, do fundraisers with their talent…" "He did stretch way beyond what a stand-up comedian does in entertainment," Nunan said. "That's a huge contribution." But the comedian's tragic death also serves as a warning of the need to deal with one's inner demons, he said.

What is at the Top?

How would you feel, when after years of sweat going through several stages in reaching the top of your field, you finally reach the top and then find nothing there? It is possible that in the process of climbing the ladder you can lose a sense of personal significance and meaning such that your professional career ceases to become a calling but just a means of making a livelihood. It is at this point that success means nothing. As successful as you become you will have failed in your search for a significant life. Building significance into life involves much more than becoming successful at what you do. Many individuals miss this distinction. They get geared up - they go through all the educational procedures, all the professional procedures to reach the top of whatever field they are tackling. Then they believe that, once they are there, significance will be a by-product of success. The truth of the matter is that significance comes from building meaning and purpose into your life, some other meaning than just being the "best and the greatest" and making the most money compared to anyone else in your field.

THE PRESSURE OF SUCCESS

Max Clifford, Britain's most high-profile celebrity publicist, shared with Reuters that stars pressure themselves to succeed. Clifford stated that "even at the top, celebrities were always worried about who could replace them." Worry, fear of failure, and the pressure to outperform their last role puts unthinkable weight on artists, which can prompt self-destructive tendencies. Clifford explained, "People assume that fame and success is all about riches and happiness but, as someone who has worked with famous people for 45 years, I know that is not the case." Clifford claims, "The success becomes like a drug to them that they have to have, and they are always worried about losing it so they push and push and work harder and harder. You have to be competitive in these fields otherwise it will not work."

IN THE FINAL ANALYSIS

Throughout your childhood and your education you've probably realized that the harder you work, the more you apply yourself to your studies and activities, and the more focused you are on achievement, the better your results are in regard to your grades, athletic or extracurricular performance, work performance, friends and family relationships. This is the one thing that will remain constant throughout your lifetime. Plain and simple, what you get out of life is a direct reflection of what you put into it. When you get together with your classmates at a ten-year class reunion, you will be amazed at the direction everyone's lives have taken. What you will discover is, those who are the most successful will be those who took control of their destiny, had a plan and pursued it with diligence and perseverance.

GET OUT OF YOUR COMFORT ZONE

People love to be in their comfort zones, once we find a particular way of doing things, we are very reluctant to change the way we go about it. If you review biographies of some of the world's most successful people, you will find a number of character traits that they all have in common. Generally these individuals have a vision—they know what they want to accomplish or what they want out of life. They set goals and they work hard to achieve them. They think positive and learn from mistakes or failures rather than using them as excuses to give up. These individuals remain focused on their objective and look for ways to overcome barriers or solve problems that would otherwise keep them from achieving what they set out to do. They are not terribly concerned about what others think of them or their ideas. Above all, they don't quit. Self-determination is a combination of skills, knowledge, and beliefs that enable a person to engage in goal-directed, self-regulated, autonomous behaviour. An understanding of one's strengths and limitations together with a belief in oneself as capable and effective are essential to self-determination. People who lead significantly successful lives use creative strategies to reach their goals. They look at options and make informed decisions. Successful planning requires that you know your responsibilities, strengths and challenges; set goals; work toward those goals; and use tools and resources available to you.

What Makes Life Worthwhile?

In 1951, at the age of 72, Albert Einstein received a letter. It moved him deeply, and caused him to reflect on what, after seven decades of living, made life worthwhile. He responded with a revealing letter. Whilst there are thousands of letters recorded, to and from the great scientist -this exchange was new, deeply personal, a rare glimpse into Einstein's judgment on the worthiness of a life well lived. So what did Einstein write? On August 24, 1951 Einstein responded: "I was really moved by your letter. It is true that the number of people striving ardently for the right and the worthwhile things is small. But the existence of these few is what makes life worthwhile."

Unfortunately life does not come with a manual. Most people struggle through life and wonder why they never get anywhere. You do not have to be one of them.

Stop Chasing Success, Seek Significance

Success influences relationships, schedules, and families. To some, it even becomes an all-consuming passion that leaves broken people and morality in its wake. Unfortunately success is not the greatest call we have on our lives because in comparison to significance, it fades quickly. Success can take up the shape and character of the prevailing economic situation. As recent years have proven, financial success is usually at the mercy of a national economy and world economy, when the economy takes a downturn, so does net worth. Success is not perpetual because it ends on the day you die. On that day, all wealth and possessions will be immediately transferred to others. The other shortcoming of success is that it is never enough. Financial success will never satisfy the inmost desires of our soul. No matter the amount of financial success earned, it always leaves us wanting more.

Significance on the other hand will always outlast you. Even when you are no longer present, your significance will still be yours and nothing can ever take that away from you. By its nature Significance carries on and keeps on giving as you positively change the life of another human being who in turn changes the life of another, who impacts the life of another and influences another. Significance also carries the capacity to satisfy our soul. While the thirst for success is never quenched, significance satisfies our deepest heart and soul. It allows us to lay our head on our pillow each night confident that we lived a valuable and fulfilling day. It is therefore unfortunate that many people spend most of their lives chasing financial success alone. While some achieve it more than others, almost all find it unfulfilling in the end. When they begin to shift their life focus to significance instead of success, they wonder why they wasted most of their life chasing something different." As we reflect on these observations and also consider the frenzied obsession of my school mates in childish pursuit of dreams of fame in a foreign land, it is important to realize that life will not last forever. You are never too young to start thinking about your legacy. How do you want people to remember you?

Is your life worth modelling after? Is it lived with character, integrity, and morality? Does your life look the same in private as it does in public? If you want to build a successful life, you make it to the top of the ladder in your field. To build a significant life you have to discover meaning and purpose along the way. You can be successful without having a significant life, but you cannot have a significant life without being successful. Success without significance is hollow.

SIGNIFICANCE DEMANDS DILIGENCE

Whatever you do, you should do energetically and enthusiastically beyond just doing it well. A person who is diligent about what they are doing gives the feeling of being responsible and willing to be held accountable for what they do. As a by-product of diligence and significance, you are blessed with success. A successful person who feels the need to tell you just how successful they are actually is telling you that their life lacks significance. You get the impression that if such people did not have all the invitations to speak, did not go to all the places they have been while doing all their important things, life would be meaningless for them. In fact, they have to tell you of all of these things so that you can be impressed with their success and your impression of their success is what gives them the little bit of significance their lives have. When there is no more applause, no more people to tell all their exploits to, these people are going to lack meaning and purpose in their lives. Significant people do not need an audience, they are too involved doing what they are doing, responding to the call upon their lives. Each of us has a deep-seated need for significance. We all long to be part of some great story in which we have an important role to play. We want to fulfil our personal destiny. This need is so deep that when people sense that their lives do not have meaning they often despair of life itself. When people use the word "calling" without acknowledging God, they are trying to find meaning in life without any basis on which to build that meaning, other than their own feelings. As you advance in life may you make progress in discovering that place - in the words of Frederick Buechner - "where your deep gladness meets the world's deep hunger."

Embrace Your Authentic Identity

Faulty foundations in self-definition and unresolved issues around personal identity can feel like a prison. They trap individuals in cycles of self-doubt, performance, and shame. One of the most destructive temptations that emerges from this place is **self-hatred**—a silent force that undermines purpose and distorts truth.

But embracing your authentic identity does not mean settling for mediocrity or ignoring areas that require growth. It means extending grace to yourself where you've fallen short, accepting where you are, and intentionally rising toward your best self—with **excellence as your standard.**

In my work with people pursuing personal transformation, I've observed a consistent thread: beneath the surface of cultural, racial, or tribal differences, many carry an inner ache that stems from living out of alignment with their true identity. Often, this originates from **unrealistic standards** imposed by systems, environments, or relationships that demand conformity at the cost of authenticity.

For some, it's easier to play roles assigned by family or culture than to pursue the person they truly desire to become. Yet living this kind of **fictional life** slowly depletes the energy needed to invest in what truly matters. It disconnects them from their deepest values and passions.

I've encountered individuals who despise nearly everything about themselves—their voice, body, hair, thoughts, and even the way they walk. They speak well of everyone else but themselves. For some, even acts of self-harm are mistakenly interpreted as moments of relief—because in their minds, they're punishing something they believe is unworthy.

Let me be clear: **self-embrace is not self-deception**. It's not ignoring your weaknesses or romanticizing failure. It's learning to forgive yourself, acknowledge where you are, and move forward with purpose and excellence. It is *being kind to your becoming.*

If your behaviour, image, or public persona is in constant conflict with your values, beliefs, passions, or true desires—it may be a sign that you are living a fictional life. In doing so, you could be silencing the very gifts and callings that were designed to shape your influence.

CONTEMPLATIVE MOMENTS:
READ AND REFLECT BEFORE ACTION.

"I cannot believe that the purpose of life is to be happy. I think the purpose of life is to be useful, to be responsible, to be compassionate. It is, above all, to matter—to count, to stand for something, to have made some difference that you lived at all." (Leo Rosten)

We place a heavy and unrealistic burden on ourselves when we try to manufacture identity and purpose solely from personal intuition. We simply weren't designed to be our own source. **Purpose flows from God.** He is both the Architect and the Author.

- Do you know your life purpose?
- Have you encountered your authentic identity beyond your roles?
- Are you aware of your assignment and spheres of influence?

Take time this week to prayerfully seek clarity from God concerning your identity, purpose, and divine assignment.

My commitments for this week: I COMMIT to _____
_____
_____

My affirmations: I AM _____
_____
_____

My transformative actions this month: I WILL _____
(1) _____
(2) _____
(3) _____

Chapter Eight

New Beginnings – Release and Let Go!

In life, the things that contaminate us the most are not necessarily agents that force themselves on us. Growing up in rural Zimbabwe herding goats, sheep and cattle - one of my greatest life lessons in those years spent with nature in solitude is that the things that damage us the most are those worthless deposits that we fail to expel from our system until they become toxic enough to destroy us at the core. Whether you have ingested abuse, betrayal or unfair treatment from an individual or organisation you need to make a choice to release it from your system before you become toxic. Release it all and allow the freshness of your Creator's promises to restore you to wholeness.

In technology, the reset button is a button or switch built into electronic devices that allows you to reset the device to its original stable settings. On a personal computer the reset button could be an actual button or concept. It would typically kick off a soft boot, instructing the computer to go through the process of shutting down, which would clear memory and reset devices to their initialized state. Generally, you would use the reset button only when a program error has caused your computer to hang.

From my experiences in herding flocks one of the most important things I learnt is that you always have to be alert of the animals' whereabouts and what pastures they are feeding from at any given time. Failure to do that could result in very grievous episodes. I used to herd a very stubborn bunch of goats that would not hesitate to stray to the nearest vegetable garden that caught their sight if you just allowed yourself to snooze for a moment. Some of these gardens would have been sprayed with poisonous insecticides. I also used to have a very notorious but exotic Brahman bull that had a knack for eating plastics. It would spend days thereafter in constipated pain until it got human assistance to expel the plastics from its system.

Dealing with Life's Stale Spots

As soon as you realise that you have hit a stale spot in your life you need to immediately begin the relentless pursuit of RE: Restructure, Refuel and Refresh to kick start your way on of your life direction. There is so much fear that is associated with refreshing one's life because of the fear of losing the things that we have accumulated and become comfortable with for so many years of our lives. Strangely some of these accumulated pieces are the very reasons why we have hit a stale spot because they have continued to weigh down so heavily upon us yet we feel that we risk losing our identity when we let them go. For some of us it could be the wounds from rejection, abuse, divorce, neglect, betrayal, false accusations and other violations to our personhood. We still want to meditate on, regurgitate and retell everyone how deeply wounded we are and somehow our recounting of the episodes of misery bring a weird consolation. We need to be very careful to separate who we are from what we have gone through. Whilst our experiences will shape our life journey by default, those same experiences do not have the authority to mould us until or unless we give them that definitive, authoritative role.

Processing Toxic Files

There are some damaged files that we keep processing in our life's central processing unit which we should have trashed out of the system days, weeks, months or decades ago. Yet sadly we continue to allow them to circulate in our system, regularly passing through our most delicate, vital and precious organs to be pumped out back again into the veins of our thoughts, feelings and emotions. Who would we really be blaming for the toxic waste we carry in our hearts and thought life? These toxic substances are responsible for the lack of wholeness we experience in our bodies and emotions which is why some of us have many hidden toes and venomous tongues and emotions that erupt at the slightest provocation. When we continue to replay files of trauma we can only expect to hallucinate even in our most wide awake moments. Naturally this intoxicated condition repels the good and well-meaning people in our lives. Even more, this paradigm will attract those things that we claim to detest and abhor the most because our state of toxicity emits certain fragrances in the intangible realm which attract the very disorder that we claim we don't want to have in our lives.

DETOXING EVERY LIFE DIMENSION

The act of erasing requires a determined effort to completely delete what you do not want to see manifesting. We cannot expect anyone to undertake that action for us because we ourselves are better acquainted with the writings that exist on the walls of our inner being. Detoxing all these life dimensions requires a boldness to confront issues and a deliberate personal effort to remove what you don't want to see in your life. The root of our contamination lies in the damaging things that we internalise and allow to take permanent residence inside of us. Once they take permanent residence in our internal realm they derail and corrupt our progress. Whilst we are not computerised devices that encounter programme errors and hang, admittedly our life processes periodically inject certain viral objects into our system. As we advance into each year in our lives, our progress or lack of it will be determined by the efforts we make to not only confront the things that have contaminated our wholeness but to delete, erase and reset our life controls for a refreshed and wholesome life.

YOU CAN RISE AGAIN!

I recently came across a very encouraging post by Dr Tonya Lyons, a General Dentist, Pastor, Mother, and Cancer Survivor:

"7 YEARS AGO TODAY I heard news that changed my life forever..."you have cancer." Little did I know that I would lose my church family, my hair, my home, my friends, my family, my weight, my eyebrows, my eyelashes, my confidence, my fingernails, my marriage, my sleep, my appetite, and my peace. What I did not lose was my MIND or my faith. God kept me and as Pastor Donald Walker, Jr preached on Easter.... No Cross No Crown. It was NEVER about me, it's not about me now. It's about YOU knowing GOD NEVER, Ever, Ever fails!! I want to invite ALL my Facebook friends to celebrate my year of COMPLETION 7yrs in Revival at The Rock tonight at 7pm!!! #carefulWHOyouleaveforDead"

I was deeply moved by her closing hash tag line #carefulWHOyouleaveforDead" because I just thought to myself that so many times we give people around us the permission to bury us before our time has come. Who have you allowed to dig your grave and bury you whilst you still have the life of God in you and a whole destiny to fulfil? Remember that Creation is waiting for you to manifest. To your Wholeness!

CONTEMPLATIVE MOMENTS:
READ THROUGH AND REFLECT BEFORE ACTION

What lingering thoughts, emotions, and inner narratives have you been recycling ever since the moment you were wounded?

What would it look like to release them—not just momentarily, but permanently?

Which habits, behaviours, or responses are no longer serving your healing—and need to be surrendered or transformed?

Who is positioned in your life to walk alongside you in this healing process—with grace, wisdom, and accountability?

*And most importantly...**Do you believe you can rise again—not as who you were, but as who you're becoming?***

My commitments for this week: I COMMIT to _____
_____
_____

My affirmations: I AM _____
_____
_____

My transformative actions this month: I WILL _____

(1) _____

(2) _____

(3) _____

The Power of RE: Restructure, Refuel and Refresh

Restructure

What do you truly want out of life?
- Where do you see yourself in 5 years' time? This is important to think about because it will give you an idea of what you want to pursue.
- If you weren't scared what would you do?
- What would you learn in order to get you to where you see yourself
- Breaking out of the mould that told you NO
  - » Who told you that?
  - » Why did you believe them?
  - » Do you think that is still true and if yes why, if no why?
  - » Are you worth pursuing that goal?
  - » If you were dying and had one opportunity to fulfil this would you still listen to the person that told you NO?

Refuel

- In the next five months, what five areas will be your main focus?
  - » No matter how ridiculous they sound to your ears, write the areas down
  - » If you achieved ALL these areas how would you feel? (Define in a short sentence how you see yourself in this area)
- Discover what fuel is good for your soul/Life
  - » What are your values and are you being true to them (write down 3 most important values in your life)
  - » Use strong affirmative language like I will or I am or I can, do not write I should, would, want. If you find this difficult—ask yourself why

Refresh

- What one area from what you have listed above would you put your heart and soul into right now?
  » What is the likelihood of success?
- What do you need to get back into perspective in your life?
- Map out all thoughts concerning this area no matter how small you think it is
  » Can you volunteer to do this? Can you shadow someone in this? What do you need to make it happen?
  » Your happiness is your responsibility—what is getting in the way of your happiness?
  » What did you learn today? Who did you love today? What made you laugh today?

Spiritual Reflections

PERFECT WHOLENESS: GOD'S ORIGINAL DESIGN FOR MAN

The Bible tells us that "the Lord God formed the man from the dust of the ground and breathed into his nostrils the breath of life, and the man became a living being." (Genesis 2:7) God created a physical body from the earth and then breathed spirit into it. The spirit gave life to the body and man became a living soul. From that point forward, humans have a spiritual nature with a soul within a physical body. God made us as complete or 'whole' beings. Each part of us is intricately interwoven with the other parts in a marvellous way. We are a masterpiece. (Ephesians 2:10) Just as the body itself is a whole unit made up of many parts (1 Corinthians 12:12), our whole self was created to function as a complete unit.

John Wesley, founder of the Methodist denomination, wrote that man was created as "a well-working system." Wesley would say that "The perfect model or expression of health would be Adam before the Fall, a balanced, harmonious, human organism designed for immortality. Since the Fall, the wholeness to be realized is wholeness within the limits of mortality." (Phillip W. Ott, John Wesley on Mind and Body: Toward an Understanding of Health as Wholeness). The Bible also tells us that God created man in his image—in the likeness of God and his Son. (Genesis 1:26) When Adam and Eve were created, they were without blemish. They had no shame because they were sinless. (Genesis 2:25)

Original Sin

When Adam and Eve sinned in the Garden of Eden, the perfect design of man was destroyed. Originally created in the image of God, this image became marred, and has been marred ever since as this image has been passed down to us all. The spirit of a person who has not been saved is dead. (Romans 5:15-17) What was once a perfectly knitted and intact spirit, soul and body became imperfect. Each of us were born into this world as flawed and imperfect beings. We inherited this from Adam and Eve. Once born physically, our soul has been subjected to all sorts of negative impact from the sin present in the world. As well, our own sins and sinful behaviours create an environment that adversely impacts on our emotional, mental and physical natures and health.

Salvation, Sanctification and Restoration

When a person accepts Jesus into their heart, they are rescued or delivered from sin and eternal separation from God. We call this salvation. The Greek word is *sozo*. God puts his Spirit into our hearts (2 Corinthians 1:22) and our spirits then become fully alive. Throughout our life on earth, our spirits will bear the image of God–*we are completely well in spirit.* We are positionally sanctified from a spiritual perspective. Acts 26:18, 1 Corinthians 1:2, 6:11, 2 Thessalonians 2:13. Salvation is the first step toward regaining complete wholeness – in mind, body and spirit—as Adam and Eve were before the fall. Although we become a "new creation" in Jesus (2 Corinthians 5:17), aspects of our self that have been tainted by sin require healing and restoration.

It is by the work of the Holy Spirit within us that we have an opportunity to progress *in our souls* toward even greater wholeness. Our marred emotions, will and thinking can be transformed by the sanctifying work of the Holy Spirit in our lives. As we surrender more and more to the Spirit of God, he can work accordingly in our lives. Sanctification is a process. We become transformed or renewed, day by day, into the likeness of Jesus. (2 Corinthians 3:18 and 4:6). Our responsibility is to purify ourselves from all that contaminates us. (2 Corinthians 7:1) We are encouraged to take an active role in "stripping off all that hinders us" (Hebrews 12:1) so that we can better bear the full image of Christ that Adam and Eve once had before they sinned. This is God's desire for us. (Romans 8:29) We are to "work out our salvation" (Philippians 2:12) that began when we were initially saved. We do this by surrendering more deeply to God. We humble ourselves and acknowledge our dependence on Him. We are more obedient to his ways. We hunger and thirst for more of Christ and we die more to our self-nature. Galatians 5:24, Luke 9:23

This is also a process of restoration, or healing, especially of our hearts. Various issues of the heart prevent us from being able to be like Jesus. Damaged emotions, belief in lies—especially of Satan's lies—and unhealed relationships all contribute to our inability to live a life like Christ—a life that fully glories God the Father. The more we allow Christ into the places of our hearts and minds, the greater opportunity we have to be restored or healed. Healing and restoration are a part of the sanctification process. The more healing we experience—especially on the inside—the more our lives will bear the fruit of the Spirit. As this occurs, our lives become a better witness or ambassador for Christ. 2 Corinthians 5:11-21.

As Dallas Willard wrote, in his book *Renovation of the Heart*, we must desire to be transformed and we must be intentional if we are to receive restoration in our soul. It will typically not just happen. Our bodies can be in varying degrees of health, wellness or state of wholeness. Even if they appear to be healthy on the outside, there may be subtle things occurring on the inside that are not well. And, I imagine that none of us have completely healthy behaviours all the time. None of us fully live out Paul's encouragement to us in Romans 12:1 – "*… I plead with you to give your bodies to God. Let them be a living and holy sacrifice—the kind he will accept. When you think of what he has done for you, is this too much to ask?*" The Apostle Paul makes it clear that our bodies groan and are burdened. 2 Corinthians 4:16-17 and 5:4 He also tells us that we eagerly await the second coming of our saviour who will then transform our 'lowly' bodies so that they will be like Jesus' 'glorious' body. As we live life on this earth, we have the opportunity to be more and more transformed into the image of Christ—the original state of Adam and Eve before the fall—with ever-increasing glory (greater wholeness). 2 Corinthians 3:18

Prayers for You

As Paul's prayer was to the Thessalonians, my prayer for you is that "God himself, the God of peace, will sanctify you through and through—in your whole spirit, soul and body…" 1 Thessalonians 5:23. I also pray that "God, who has begun a good work within you, will continue *his work* (restoration, healing and transformation) until it is finally finished on the day when Christ Jesus returns." Philippians 1:6. Amen.

About the Author

Cynthia Chirinda is a Transformation Catalyst, Systems Change Practitioner, and Personal Development Coach committed to guiding individuals and institutions toward wholeness, purpose, and sustainable impact. With a background in communications, leadership, and organizational development, she blends strategic insight with spiritual depth to support healing, growth, and generational leadership.

Cynthia has served across diverse sectors—from grassroots communities to policy tables—as a facilitator of restorative dialogue, talent development, and visionary thinking. She is the founder of **Wholeness Incorporated** and **Women Politicians Incubator Zimbabwe (WOPIZ)** and has played a catalytic role in civic engagement and capacity development throughout Africa.

She is the author of over a dozen transformational books, including *The Whole You*, *Can the Whole Woman Please Stand Up!*, *Managing Transitions*, *The Connection Factor Series*, and the *You Are Not Damaged Goods* series. Her literary works, coaching programs, and speaking platforms continue to inspire authenticity, emotional healing, and values-driven leadership.

Cynthia is also the visionary behind initiatives such as:
- **Intelligent Conversations with Cynthia**—a broadcast platform sparking faith-based, leadership, and healing dialogues;
- **The Extra Mile**—a film tribute to women building nations;
- and **Women Rising in Africa**—a multimedia series spotlighting African women leaders.

She believes that wholeness is not about perfection, but about alignment—becoming rooted in faith, refined by life, and responsive to divine purpose.

Connect with Cynthia
Email: info@cynthiachirinda.com
Website: www.cynthiachirinda.com
LinkedIn: Cynthia Chirinda

Suggested Resources & Inspirations
The following works and voices have helped shape parts of my journey and message in this book:
- Clinton, J. R. *The Making of a Leader* (1988). NavPress.
- Faith and Health Connection: *Understanding the Connection Between Spirituality and Health* (www.faithandhealthconnection.org)
- Dete, M. (2008). *Let it Rain, May Blessings Come*. Harare, Zimbabwe.
- Hagin, K. W. *Christ: The Bread of Life*.

Thank You for Reading
If this book has resonated with your journey, I'd love to hear from you. Share your reflections, testimony, or personal breakthrough by connecting with me:
Email: info@cynthiachirinda.com
Website: www.cynthiachirinda.com
Socials: Tag your post with **#DestinationWholeness** to share how the message impacted you.

Look out for *The Destination Wholeness Guided Journal*—A companion tool to deepen your reflection, track transformation, and walk in intentional healing.

Stay connected for updates via newsletter or social platforms.

www.ingramcontent.com/pod-product-compliance
Lightning Source LLC
Chambersburg PA
CBHW081329190426
43193CB00044B/2897